Resurrection Party

Resurrection Party
poems

Michalle Gould

SILVER BIRCH PRESS
LOS ANGELES, CALIFORNIA

© COPYRIGHT 2014, Michalle Gould, ALL RIGHTS RESERVED

ISBN-13: 978-0692258316

ISBN-10: 0692258310

FIRST EDITION: September 2014

Email: silver@silverbirchpress.com

Web: silverbirchpress.com

Blog: silverbirchpress.wordpress.com

Cover art: "Danse Macabre" by Michael Wolgemut (1493).

Mailing Address:
Silver Birch Press
P.O. Box 29458
Los Angeles, CA 90029

Resurrection Party

FOR
Those who came before
Those who are now
and Those who will come after

Poems

I

How Not to Need Resurrection / 14
The Angels Discuss the Attribution of Michelangelo's
    "Creation of Adam" / 15
We Were Never Angels / 16
Revelation by Water / 17
Where there are doors, there are colors of doors . . . / 18
Self-Portrait as a Rare Book Exhibited at a Museum in England / 19
In the dreams of the Venus de Milo . . . / 20
Self-Portrait as a Series of Preparatory Studies for a Nude
    by Matisse / 21

II

Brontide / 24
When I Was Naked / 25
Hamlet / 26
When I Fell to Earth / 27
Evidence of Human Remains / 28
Untitled / 29
On the Potential Appearance of Resurrection / 30
Signs / 31

III

Landscape with Exotic Animals / 34
Anthropodysmorphia / 35
Self-Portrait as the Time Distance Between Us / 36
Spring Awakening / 37
Wild Things / 38
Self-Portrait as a Pair of Lovebirds / 39
Self-Portrait as the Maiden of Athens / 40
Epitaph & Testament / 41

IV

Revelation by Fire / 44
After the Fall / 45
The Surrender Field / 46
Square / 47
Rectangle / 48
Medusa's Head / 49

V

Tonight, the clouds / 52
New England Boarding School: Winter / 53
Rehearsing Lear (for the school play) / 54
Riddle on Metamorphosis / 55
Absolution / 56
Chastity / 57
Self-Portrait as a Message from Rapunzel to the Princes Trying to Rescue Her / 58
Postlude (when I was invisible) / 59

VI

Ordeal by Cross / 62
Revelation / 63
I am the architect (not the builder) / 64
Dirge for a Dinosaur by Its Bones / 66
Self-Portrait as an Ampoule of Martyr's Blood Buried with Them in Their Tomb / 67
The Prophet Resigns / 68
Words from a Pound of Flesh / 69
What It Means to Be Alive at the Time of the Resurrection of the Dead / 70

I died, and death is neuter; it speaks not, it gives no answer.

—The Risen Lord, D.H. Lawrence

We die with the dying:
See, they depart, and we go with them.
We are born with the dead:
See, they return, and bring us with them.

—Little Gidding, T.S. Eliot

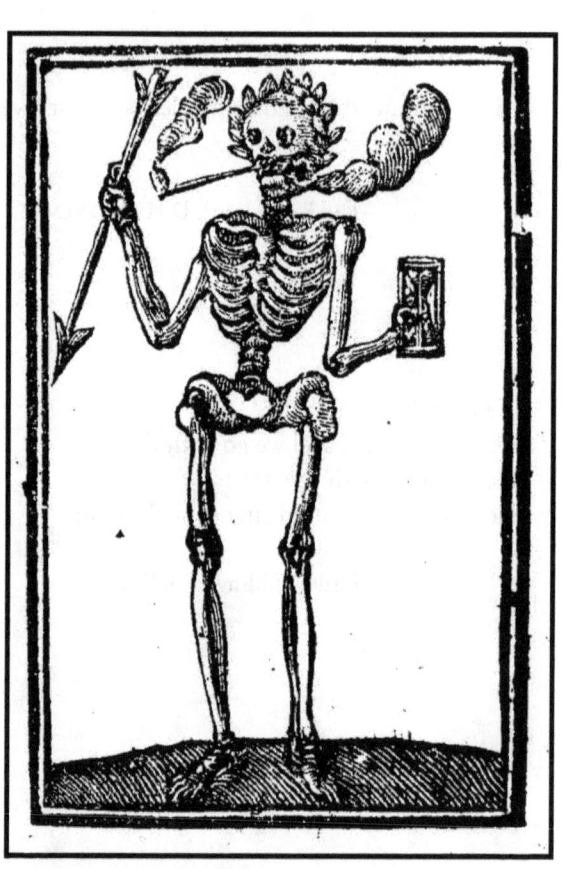

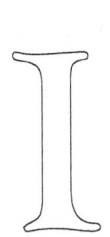

How Not to Need Resurrection

Children like to play at death—
they hold their breath,
and cross their arms and shut their eyes
until they forget to be dead; then rise
from their nest of pillows and play instead
at being lost or married,
as if their state was mutable, as if, like water
they could flow or freeze or climb without a ladder
into the heavens then drop back down—
they are the first resurrectionists, they alone
understand the trick is *not* to try,
that once you believe in death, you must surely die.

The Angels Discuss the Attribution of
Michelangelo's "Creation of Adam"

Who is the master of *this* landscape,
this fleshly man-scape, its earth-toned
protuberances and shadowed valleys, sunken
and etched with tiny lashes of dirty color?
The draftsmanship, although beautiful, lacks that dimensional
quality achieved by our Master's hand.
The staffage lacks liveliness, the figure does not spring
from the stretched altar from which it's offered,
does not extend unmuted hand to its creator,
does not say, "I am." I am not, it weeps
(even its tears are thin as paper),
but the mere image of a man.

We Were Never Angels

> There were Nephilim on the earth in those days . . .
> Genesis 6:4

We just looked the part. Taller, bigger, stronger.
Blonder. We spread the story around to get women—
For all we knew, there was no god. The heavens fierce
And distant in their immaculate virginity,
The great tower never pierced them, so far a fall would kill
    anyone.
We have visited Babel's ruins, seen the great heap
Of dust, I once brought a woman there. "*See,*" I told her,
"*We are on the same team, you and I.*"
We linked hands to spit at the sky. "Our sons will build ships
To launch an attack upwards," she said.
But my seed was rotten, like the rest of me,
My tongue swells with each lie, the water joins
With strangeness (the dust I swallowed with her body)
And stops my mouth, my back attaches
To the earth, my eye cast upward, toward that darkling ship,
That tar-caked vessel casting its malevolent shadow,
So I cannot even see the sun through the gathered waters.
I will never return in glory to those cloud-kept pastures.
It is a strange dream that has no waking in it.

Revelation by Water
    (Narcissus)

At my birth, the midwife cried her delight:
"Not even a god has eyes like this!"
She said. My mother clapped, my father cursed
The half-drawn curtain that let Apollo's kiss
Enter at dawn to raise a blush on her belly,
Unpeeling lengths of lemon skin and rind
Of orange and all among them cherry
To contest paternity, to wind
Into a crevice and plant fruit
That would be born during the spring
When youth's ardor is all-admiring
Towards my flaming eyes,
Like two suns in one sky only I
Have never seen, asking, "Where is a glass?"
"A glass," whispers the wind as it passes
Over the pool, but my eye
Does not reflect back from that mirror;
Instead, it shows only the double image
Of a faultless milk and golden flower—
As if Heaven itself was an egg
lying broken in half there.

Where there are doors, there are colors of doors . . .

Once you've opened yours, you must paint it a blue
Perhaps with an undertone of *surprising lemon,*
In which, if you peer very closely,
You might find occasional spots of *pale blanched orange—*
Far from the pure blue you'd find in a child's palette,
Those eight discs they use to portray the world in uncomplicated
    brightness;
We didn't get "*the color of salt that has been in the sea*"
Until at least middle school. "*The color of salt
That has been too long in the sea*" came much much later,
After the house had been painted "*the color of an apple
With a worm inside of it,*" using highlights of "*William Blake's
The Sick Rose*" and lowlights of "*a heart that will be broken twice,*"
But it's just red anyway, no matter what they say,
Just bright red and dark red and red with a touch of purple,
As there is little difference between "*the blue that is the color
Of a lover's eyes*" and "*the blue that is the color of the water
After it smoothes over the spot where a stone has sunk beneath it.*"
This tells you not a thing about blue, nothing, not anything
    at all,
Although if (and only if) it was "*the blue that is the color
Of your lover's eyes, that is like the color of the water
Just after it smoothes over the spot where a person has sunk beneath it,*"
That might tell us more than we wanted to know about
    your lover

Self-Portrait as a Rare Book Exhibited at a Museum in England

Every few days, they turn the page.
They never ask me first, nor if I mind
the crowds that gape at where I lie
in this glass cage; these look, but then move on—
they do not think of me again,
after they're done, except for one . . .
He seems to seek to know me not in part
but as I am in full, returning to study me
in this incremental fashion, like some Salome
unveiled, inch by inch, limb by limb.
Perhaps, once the end is reached,
he might unlock this box and set me free.
Then I would ask him to take me home,
to dwell on a shelf in his own library—
where only his hand could open me.

In the dreams of the Venus de Milo . . .

The earth gives endless birth to hands
she can not shake or grasp.
Oh drowning men, you must await
another savior. Clasp
her ankle though you might
she will elude you. Her babies
dot the landscape, she must find
a way to save each
one. How might she raise them
to the breast her husband
bared before he laid her down,
took tool in hand
and forged that beauty of immortal charm
that now gnaws and bites and chews through the ground
in search of each amputated arm.

*Self-Portrait as a Series of Preparatory Studies for
a Nude by Matisse*

The breasts hang low like fruit hoping
to be picked yet still on the branch,
While the body largely reclines, a letter K
lain on its side and slightly bent,
or in a less common pose, my back faces the viewer
so I resemble a pushed in O, my arms and legs drawn in,
like a turtle withdrawing far into its shell
to escape some predator that has come to suck;
We are become a rock. Our hearts lie hidden far
Below its skin. The artist scrapes my flesh onto his brush
but cannot touch what lies beneath, whatever he thinks—
nor can you, my dear, even as you read me.

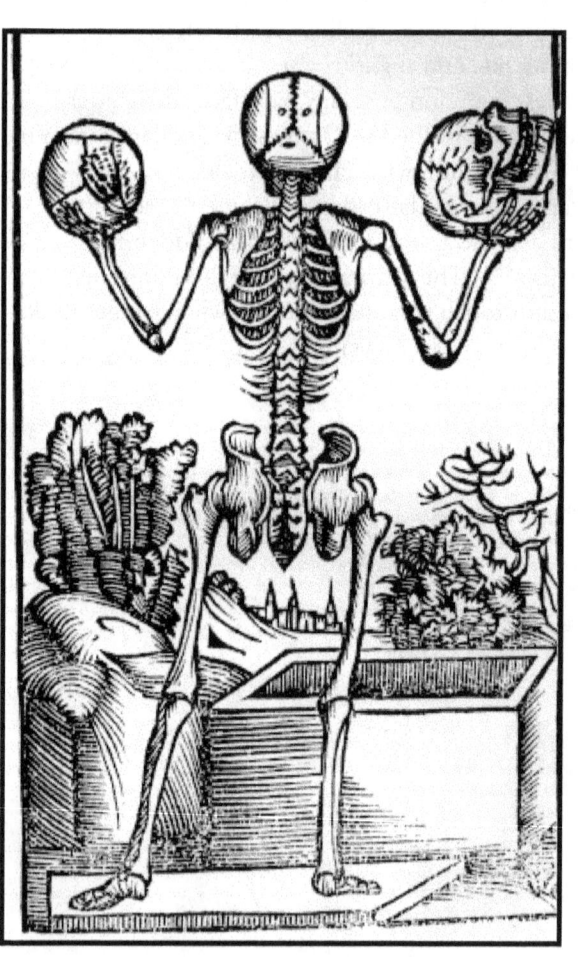

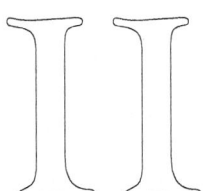

Brontide

: a low muffled sound like distant thunder heard in certain
seismic regions esp. along seacoasts and over lakes and thought
to be caused by feeble earth tremors

A melancholy sennet announcing movement—
A slow struggling form of levitation,
In which no magician wields his powers,
Where no trick is possible, no sleight of hand,
Only the earth itself, drowned and naked,
Coming to meet us, as all spirits do,
with a faint howl of greeting, intended to ensure
that we know to expect them, to avoid our being surprised
or made frightened by their arrival—if only there was
someone to translate, someone to explain to us
that this was what these sounds meant!

When I Was Naked

I was the sturdy bowl of plums half-buried in snow
outside the artist's studio. He paints the shades of purple
reflected in condensed water on my skin.

I was the snowy hill topped by a nun's black habit,
a fall of dark hair descending to wintry shoulders,
an infinite stretch of icy skin.

My body was a mystery. The anatomist
touched his scalpel to the edge of my jaw,
opened his sketchpad and drew back my skin.

A courtesan in Osaka tried something new, trimmed away
    leaves,
stem, floated me—denuded lily—in a stone bowl full of milk.
A day later, the bowl was scattered petals on a blue-white skin.

A vine is a humble creeping thing, but clustered in boastful
    fruit.
We called to the artist, "I am emerald! I am amethyst!"
until some wild animal left us naked, eating only our skin.

In a cemetery, a mole tunneled back and forth between the
    graves,
extended blind fingers, knew before any scientist,
the last to go is hair. The first is skin.

Hamlet

All the dead in *Hamlet* die on stage, but one:
Ophelia, caught between the wings
and the make-up room. The water has her up
against the wall Ophelia never will see a nunnery,
but chants old hymns, as one who never read the book
and doesn't know the way the story ends.
The water lifts her skirts to fill them, as Hamlet never did,
holds her aloft in a fist half drawn to mercy,
as if regretting the dirty work left to be done,
so by the time her final moments come,
the final scene onstage has already begun;
the water spits Ophelia out like half chewed meat
too tough to swallow, leaves her a heap of sodden rags
discarded on the theatre floor, trash by the river's shore.

As for the rest, the water sweeps onstage and takes
them one by one, extends wet fingers along the coast
to England, embraces even minor characters,
as poems too often fail to do, takes as an extra prize
Horatio too, so no one is left to greet young Fortinbras,
the prince of Norway, who although a soldier, took lessons
with military precision, knows not only Shakespeare
but old English myth ur-Hamlet, memorized
his lines, takes in the floating carnage on the stage,
and says, as planned, *Where is this sight?*, then waits,
and waits, and says, *There is no line for this*, and though
the audience bids him speak, is still, and will not speak again.

When I Fell to Earth

I was a chewed up piece of planet two gods
tried to pass from mouth to mouth and dropped

I was a kind of damaged star, broken off
from the force of their heavenly coupling

I was a bit of sport, a meteor, a ball
in a game played far above your heads

I was a misdirected ship that could not beat
my way back into the sky,

I was a painted wooden bird that could not unmake
a present of myself

I was a flood that could not find an ocean
large enough to consume me

I tried to unwake my fall, but could not find
a dreamer strong enough to take me

And each time I fell, I wept, I said, my god
from up here they look so small, so small

Evidence of Human Remains

I was the dune in the Mexican desert
A pilot mistook for a replica of the Pyramids,
The wind brushing ripples across my surface,
As if I were not sand but water.

I was the lake birthed by the intercourse of five rivers.
A forgotten king named me the palm
And these rivers the fingers of god.
An outstretched hand of water.

I was the plane brought up from the sea,
Bearing no evidence of human remains.
Two days later, a fisherman pried a glass eye
From an oyster. Blue, like water.

I was the Mississippi, when I burst my banks.
The clouds mistook the roofs of submerged houses
For barges floating on the river.
The roofs mistook the clouds for faces, reflected back from
    water.

I was the mingling of blues in a painting
Called *The Hour of Sadness/The Hour of Gladness:*
When the pillars holding the Heavens will be broken
And the sky will fall, born again as water.

Untitled

This was supposed to be a landscape without a person in it,
but there you are—that tree slouches the way you do.
Periodically, it drops something it has no way to pick up.
It does not weep now, but at any moment,
there is the capacity for weeping in it,
and those leaves! Those broad green leaves, shaped like hearts
someone has cut from the wrong color of paper, so large a target
it's almost impossible not to pluck them.
They are wounded, then lost, then there they are again!
It must be nice to have such an endless capacity for renewal.
Well, man is made from earth, I suppose, which is limitless,
while we are just one rib, the smallest, the most breakable.
I might return it to you, if I could, if it would make you whole,
but then again, I might not, because you are just the landscape,
and where would you be without I—the one that creates you?

On the Potential Appearance of Resurrection

It will come like the day to some child
who doesn't understand time, who—arising
in the middle of the night—thinks a thief
stole the sun, sees the morning's wild
entrance as a miracle beyond imagining,
the return of something so lost that he didn't even dare
pray for its homecoming—like that time
when you find yourself both loving
and loved simultaneously—that rare,
                        that astonishing.

Signs

Leaves beat like hands against the windowpane,
A crowd of visitors eager to gain entry,
But where is their tree?

Will you marry me tattooed in white ink
Upon the sky's broad back, but where is the plane hiding
And who is the addressee?

The end is nigh proclaims a sign left in the middle of the road,
The rapture approaches, but where is the prophet?
Taken away to heaven?

Perhaps the end is already here.

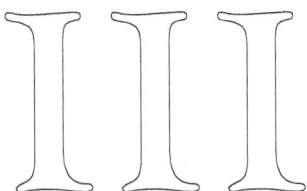

Landscape with Exotic Animals

Was the name we gave our cloud formation.
But then I fell, and the whole procession soon accompanied me,
so sorry to see me go that they wept fat irregular tears—
the camel cried away his lump, the wailing elephant
his trunk and half an ear. I cried, "Catch me, I'm falling!"
How we laughed, how we laughed. I said, "Look, it's not so far,"
tried to pretend I wasn't bursting (but how it hurt, how it hurt!).
"Look," I said, "I'll meet you down there—we'll accumulate
    together."
With only my mouth left of my imitation of a monkey,
my water painfully broken, I shouted, "One day we'll be clouds
    again."

"Next time," I shouted, "next time, we'll form *Landscape with the
    Fall of Icarus!*"

Anthropodysmorphia
    informed by Lewis Thomas's *Lives of a Cell: Notes of a Biology Watcher*

When will this face launch even a single ship?
One sees them flying past, but knows not where
their travels take them, nor the port that gave them up.

Oh Helen, lend me your beauty! Or should I rather take as
    tutor
the less immortalized lady moth, whose pheromones could
    summon
a trillion suitors, were they deployed at once.

Her mates are drawn to her scent across great distance
to find her in the night. Whereas, to communicate,
termites beat their heads against the floors of their nests, in the
dark,
                                            as we also do.

Self-Portrait as the Time Distance Between Us

Even when I glimpse you for a moment, my tongue is stilled as speech deserts me, while a delicate fire is beneath my skin . . .
SAPPHO

My own tongue is spurred by absence—
Your evening, my afternoon; my sun, your moon.
Your morning, my broken rest; your movements wake me
as if we were asleep in the same bed.
Your chill creeps through my open window
Like a thief, to pick my pocket,
Leaving a trail of wet behind it,
Whose cause I have forgotten,
By the time I next wake,
Like a dream deliberately left unrecorded,
For the sake of that unexpected shock of pleasure,
when some chance association
Causes it to be remembered
Suddenly later that same day.

Spring Awakening

A bird proclaimed upon a branch
To all the world its joy—
A boy that loved a pretty girl,
Or a girl a pretty boy?

I stopped to watch it singing there,
Like Hardy's darkling thrush.
It dove to bite me on the cheek
And left a dar(l)ing flush.

Wild Things

My bed is warm tonight.
And spare. A length of wood.
A mat of grass. And hair.
Some animal is bare,
tonight, under my bed.
Its fur embraces my
body. I arch my back
and sigh. It licks its lips.
The skin slips off my toes.
Tonight, are you hungry?
Nibble away, oh monster.
My dreams await. Meet me there.

Self-Portrait as a Pair of Lovebirds

Opening their beaks, they thrust
their tongues out for one last kiss
before the long journey south—

like worms they each intend to drop
into the other's hungry waiting mouth.

Self-Portrait as the Maiden of Athens

That day, I went forth to kill the Minotaur.
Since Theseus, they sent us all naked;
I had no ball of string; I had no sword.
For tools, instead, I had only the instruments
of my body: my nails for daggers, my hair for thread.
I had heard of his legendary cruelty;
I had heard how he killed without a word.
Then I came to the center and saw him.
His strong arms beckoned—and I cut the cord.

Epitaph & Testament

Love me now—for I am dead—
And shroud me in a dress of red,
or blue, whichever you prefer—
so long as I don't look like her . . .

Hold me now—for I am dead—
And drop your kisses on my head,
or anywhere that you'd prefer—
so long as you're not kissing her . . .

Eat my eyes and drink my blood,
And weave my hair into a rug . . .
Build a cage out of my ribs,
Where only your heart and mine shall live.

And if she tries to climb inside?
Use my teeth to bite her hide . . .

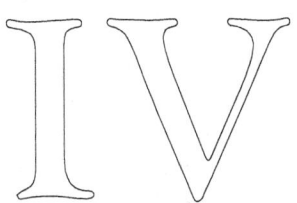

Revelation by Fire
(Comfort, Texas)

Speak to me, tree,
your leaves swollen into illuminated circles,
like many-autumned lightbulbs . . .
like gaudy ornaments that thief Winter
forgot, here where the earth is full of color,
as if a cathedral had released its windows
to stain the ground around them.
A man left in a well by his brothers
does not question the driver of the next caravan.
This is how you become a slave in a distant land.
Tree, I know you tire of your burden.
Your leaves grow engorged with color,
even their stems warming red—
like breasts too heavy with milk—
if you cannot release them, let me pluck them.
What a round ball of fire I now clutch
between my hands, like a small burning bush
cupped to warm them! Any caravan
will do in this desert. A single man
quickly becomes a congregation.
That boy holds a burst of flame threatening
to lick his lip. Oh tree! May I take it from him?

After the Fall

I was a rain in sere conditions,
consumed by the dry and the dust,
too soon forgotten by the heaven
from which I'd fallen, a crust

of earth rushed to cover me over;
it formed no pillow to greet my head.
I am like rust on the hinge of a door,
I am the very heel of a loaf of bread.

The Surrender Field
(after John Donne)

Like troops laying siege to a city
I made war on your heart.
Believing you would admit me
Soon enough, I watched the rampart
For some flag of surrender,
For some sign from within
That you wished to be overthrown.
But no sign did I find there,
Having no supplies for the winter,
I was forced to depart for home;
Forgive me—I did not wish to enter
By force, or await any longer
Reinforcements that would not come

Square

The symmetry of a square
is somehow more terrifying
than that of a circle
or even a perfect triangle

A circle is warm and inviting
you want to fill it with something

A triangle is whimsical,
the kind of joke that's already funny,
even before you hear the punch line

But the square stands alone:
neither asking nor giving
a mirror reflecting nothing

Rectangle

The most open of all the shapes,
even drawn in two dimensions

the square and triangle
are stuck to the page

a circle is, at best, a hole,

but a rectangle—
a rectangle is a door

or an elevator,
going somewhere

Medusa's Head

was eventually too dangerous
to keep around

where drops of blood fell
from her slighted neck,
snakes would spring from the ground

it kept turning the wrong things to stone:

an important spring, a minor god,
a young seamstress Zeus had his eye on

even his sword could not penetrate that mortified flesh

as revenge, he had the head confined
to a mostly empty room

trapped in eternal contemplation of her own image
in a mirror

her own petrified face

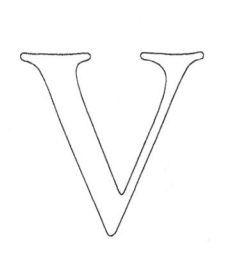

Tonight, the clouds

Tonight, the clouds
Are tired of flying
Above the earth

Like hostages,
Suspended by chains
They long for rest

They long for the day
When the ground
Will accept them

They will sleep
On its surface
In pools of puddled white

In their place
The heavens will be strewn
With lawns of grass

New England Boarding School: Winter

Snow is a country doctor,
making its house call at night,
as if something cannot wait,
as if someone must be born, or
have their death made easier.
Letting itself out from the sky,
that black leather bag too high
and too wide to measure,
snow makes itself a newfangled x-ray machine,
revealing a house as a tent
atop a box, a tree as an outline
of an up-thrust arm and spread-out hand.
Only the sea resists its work, proclaiming
"I am like nothing except what I am."

Rehearsing Lear
(for the school play)

He is afraid the glass will swallow him,
as teachers sometimes do their students.
But that way madness lies, he says, watching
his face transform into another's face,
tearing his clothes: *Off, off, you lendings!*
He begs his eyes to threaten tears. Summoned,
they are dismissed once they arrive,
Like some servant called to perform a task
the master has meanwhile himself accomplished.
No, he says. I will weep no more.
The mirror reflects his nakedness—too young
to know this madness in its form as found in nature,
un-knowing later that night in the audience
he could find the faces of many franker teachers.

Riddle on Metamorphosis

To be human is to be like a cloud chalked into the sky
    that some eraser could sweep off the blue board at any moment
To be immortal is to be solid as a pear in an old Dutch still life
    that would choke you if you tried to swallow it, no matter
how small your bite
But what does it mean to be a cloud shaped like that pear?

There are two kinds of sacredness often ascribed to a saint's body,
either its lack of decay or its absence altogether from the grave
As you never see the skeleton, the cloud has no bones to rustle
but simply shifts: becoming a turtle or a tablet of bread, whose pieces fall
Not to feed but to instruct, naked and particular in shape as we must learn to be

Absolution

As the sidewalk forgives my feet
for their lack of apology,
so the sky forgives the mountain,
for reaching through a cloud
to stick the heavens,
drawing a few bright drops of liquid
like a brooch that in piercing a dress
accidentally breaches the skin.
The city forgives the map
for betraying its secrets . . .
its houses wear their roofs
like pointed hats
for a party thrown to show
it has forgiven me
for leaving it

Chastity

Virtue, you claim, is its own reward,
and needs no answering prize.
Yet doesn't anything of worth,
hope to be recognized?
Just beware lest you become
much like the sorry miser,
who retreats from the world
to count his coin,
and emerges to a new currency,
and all its value gone.

Self-Portrait as a Message from Rapunzel to the Princes Trying to Rescue Her

Build me a city, or burn it,
I do not care.
If you don't stop trying to save me,
I will cut my hair.

Postlude (when I was invisible)

Footprints stain the newly poured concrete
outside a church. A black hat
lies forgotten in the middle of a street
outside a mosque where dark men meet in clusters,
their women ignoring the wicked wind
that steals its way into their scarves. Lucky pickpocket!
I am that breeze, escaping,
clutched in my brazen grasp,
a few strands of precious hair . . .
I am the summoning
to morning prayer.

VI

Ordeal by Cross

"Lift your arms up, lad,"
said the jailer. "Lift them up!"
The boy was accused of stealing,
but proclaimed his innocence.
"You have to keep them up!"
the jailer told him. He went
the next morning to his trial
by ordeal. He and his accuser
would stretch their arms out
on either side of a cross; the first
to lower his arms lost. The boy's
opponent was a knight and very
strong. The jailer knew the lad
would go to the grave
as the others before him had.
But "God will give me the strength,"
the boy said. This was what
was supposed to happen if
your cause was just. Some twist
of fate would come; the knight,
although greater in strength,
would be struck by a fever,
or trip over a rock, or feel the need
to defecate. "You should yield,"
the jailer advised the boy,
"If you are losing." He would be fined
and lose his freedom, but he would live.
"But as I am not guilty," said the boy,
"Surely God will save me? Besides,
if I lose, and am hanged,
and they bury me,
once it has been three days,
as I am innocent,
might I not also come back?"

Revelation

The prophet stands ready
to receive the word of God at all times:
his mind empty, a tent in need only of a guest,
its door always cracked open . . .

While his body is like a bag never fully unpacked,
a word commonly used
standing at the tip of the tongue,
in preparation to be spoken.

As a consequence, the prophet must
too often be away from his people:
Traveling to a desert, or returning home from a mountaintop—
But someone has to save the world.

Nonetheless, he hates having to tell them what to do;
He'd rather converse about their families,
Or maybe elephants,
Or anything aside from blood and lightning.

Why can't I say something positive for a change?
He asks, like, "Nice job not worshipping any idols . . .
This week," or, "Don't be so hard on yourself.
At least you didn't murder anybody."

He would like to have a dog.
If only he could just keep it to himself,
He would obey God's commands:
Build an ark, feed the angels.

Why can't a single man be sufficient
To save any two condemned cities?
But perhaps he is just envious.

Perhaps he too would like the chance to believe,
Or not to, as in their place, having never been so fortunate
Or unfortunate as to see the back of God's face.

I am the architect (not the builder)
(after Ghalib)

The unfinished house opens everywhere;
pigeons squat along its beams.
My toolbox lies open and empty.

Not much chance of snow to the weatherman,
but when tears froze from his eyes, I thought to protect the
    house,
standing uncovered and empty.

I traveled by hot air balloon, but the winds were too strong—
they tried to carry me past.
I parachuted out, leaving the gondola empty.

I had thought to cut the balloon from its basket,
lash it tight to the uprights, drape it over the rafters,
put a roof where the rise waited, empty.

Did I think myself that god who makes snakes out of sticks,
to make a woman's hair of the balloon draped around the
    building's face,
now left unadorned and empty?

The snow comes heaven-faced like a bride.
It cleaves to the nakedness of the frame.
The pigeons have left us. The house is quiet and empty.

I am no maker of arks. I should not have dared to build
    anything.
My knees are bruised.
I would pray, but my mouth is dried out and empty.

I hoped only to put a resting place in this far field,
on the way up the mountain. Instead pilgrims pause as they
    pass it,
but move on when they see it lies empty.

For years I have watched, longing always to join them,
but my house needed finishing. Now they have all gone
    before me,
the tombstones shoved aside—the graves lying empty.

Dirge for a Dinosaur by Its Bones

Longing impresses itself
into the form of the world
that surrounds it; replicating
itself physically, in the image
of the objects found nearest it.
We are haunted not by a ghost,
but its corporeal incarnation,
as a wound sometimes reminds us
by its shape of the very instrument
of its creation. As, yesterday,
during installation at the museum,
our shadow grew upon the wall,
until we seemed for a moment to be
(re-assembled at last after such long separation)
joined there once more to that same flesh
which failed to prevent our extinction.

Self-Portrait as an Ampoule of Martyr's Blood Buried with Them in Their Tomb

I was sealed in flame.
A red crown burning bright
around my head. I was anointed.
Promised that I would live again.
In darkness, I waited. Like a turnip
consigned to a cellar to endure the winter.
Inside me, the blood hardened.
A strange form of calcification.
Some say to live at all is a form of martyrdom.
Any heart is an ampoule of blood
entombed inside a human body,
A vial, a closed coffin made of glass.
To open us, you must snap our necks.

The Prophet Resigns

When you come to the field, my friend,
I may not be there.
But the corn has ears larger than mine.

And though when you descend to the mountaintop,
you may not find me,
some bird will circle round, if you give it time.

Only sand and the illusion of sand
will wait for you in the desert.
But a caravan or the illusion of a caravan always eventually
    passes by.

If we long for each other, we must remember
that though Sarah was twice forced to pretend to be Abraham's
    sister,
not even for a moment did she actually cease to be his wife.

Words from a Pound of Flesh

The scale expects me. But whether to accumulate
in its loose and cold embrace in scraps and ounces,
or to pulse as a single heaving mass, awaiting word
as to the appropriateness of my size, I do not know.

I would prefer some other task: directing the flow
of blood like scarlet rivers through this body. Or conducting
the digestive functions by which it purges and renews itself:
like the burning of old wood and fertilization of seeds in some
    great forest.

But I was never named, neither heart nor kidney nor lung
nor stomach, nor any other part belonging to a man.
I might like to know my place. A brain serves a different
    function
than a liver, which is categorized separately from a clavicle.

But however sorted: whether lymphatic, or skeletal, or
    muscular—
are we not yet one body?

*What It Means to Be Alive at the Time of the Resurrection
of the Dead*

No one tells you it's here.
A perfunctory knock on the door
awaits no answer, they enter
and crowd at your table, their
boots are damp and spore-
ridden. "Hard work," says your father,
"Being dead. If you could bring some water?"
"But what was it *like*?" you ask, unhappy to have missed it,
alone among your family. Your mother sighs,
like a girl remembering her lover,
"Different than I expected." In her wrist
the blood runs again—a boy at school once bit all the girls there,
except you, because the bell rang. How you cried that night
in your bed! As if you hadn't been kissed.

ACKNOWLEDGMENTS

Poems from "Resurrection Party" first appeared in the following journals: "How Not To Need Resurrection" and "What It Means To Be Alive at the Time of Resurrection" in *Poetry*, "The Angels Discuss the Attribution of Michelangelo's *The Creation of Adam*" (as "Attribution") and "Where there are doors, there are colors of doors" in *New England Review*, "We Were Never Angels" in *Pleiades*, "When I Was Naked" in *North American Review*, "Hamlet" in *Beloit Poetry Journal*, "Evidence of Human Remains *(when I was big)*" in *Slate*, "On the Potential Appearance of Resurrection" in *NA Literary Journal*, "Signs" in *Little Red Leaves*, "Riddle on Metamorphosis" in *Womb*, "Postlude *(when I was invisible)*" in *MWU!*, and "Dirge for a Dinosaur by Its Bones" in *American Literary Review*. Thank you to the editors of these journals for publishing them! In addition, several of these poems appeared in my chapbook, *Resurrection Party*, published in 2007 by Michelle Detorie's Hex Presse.

I am grateful to David Wevill, Judith Kroll, Heather McHugh and Talvikki Ansel for their guidance and feedback during my time at the Michener Center for Writers at the University of Texas-Austin, as well as Jim Magnuson, Marla Akin, and Bruce Snider for their administration of the Michener Center program at the time I attended (1998-2001).

In particular, thank you to my friends and family for their long and patient support of my writing.

ABOUT THE AUTHOR

Michalle Gould has been working on the poems that constitute this collection for almost fifteen years. In that time, her poems and short stories have been published in *Slate, New England Review, Poetry, American Literary Review, The Texas Observer*, and other journals. She currently lives in Los Angeles, where she works as a librarian, and is in the process of researching and writing a novel set in the North of England during the 1930s.

www.ingramcontent.com/pod-product-compliance
Lightning Source LLC
Chambersburg PA
CBHW070629050426
42450CB00011B/3153